THE
ELECTORAL
COLLEGE:

Critical to Our Republic

T0204757

JOSIAH PETERSON

with a prologue by Thomas H. Patrick

THE
KING'S
COLLEGE
PRESS

The King's College Press is the book-publishing division of the liberal arts Christian college, The King's College, featuring scholarly works by The King's College staff, faculty, and alumni. Through its commitment to the truths of Christianity and a biblical worldview, The King's College seeks to transform society by preparing students for careers in which they help to shape and eventually lead strategic public and private institutions, and by supporting faculty members as they directly engage culture through writing and speaking publicly on critical issues.

Cover design: Natalie Nakamura

ISBN 978-0-692-89695-2

Published in the United States by:

The King's College Press
56 Broadway
New York, NY, 10004
www.tkc.edu

For Thomas H. Patrick,
who makes so much at The King's College possible

Contents

Five Myths about the Electoral College

MYTH 1: The Electoral College was an accident, an unprincipled compromise made by the Constitution's Framers.

TRUTH: The Electoral College was a brilliant and principled solution to a problem confronting the Framers. The Framers crafted a system that not just three-quarters of the states were—but every state was—willing to accept and that reinforced two key principles: the separation of powers and federalism. (*See page 7*)

MYTH 2: The Electoral College violates the democratic principles of the founders.

TRUTH: Our founders sought to make America a republic, reflecting the consent of the governed through representative government and the rule of law. (*See page 16*)

MYTH 3: The Electoral College is racist.

TRUTH: The modern Electoral College aims neither to advantage nor disadvantage any specific race. (*See page 20*)

MYTH 4: The Electoral College always favors conservatives.

TRUTH: The Electoral College also helped presidents Bill Clinton, Woodrow Wilson, Harry Truman, and John F. Kennedy validate their elections. (*See page 42*)

MYTH 5: The Electoral College unfairly favors less populous states over more populous ones.

TRUTH: High population states enjoy a big advantage in the House of Representatives and still maintain most of the power in presidential elections. Along with the Senate, the Electoral College provides a counterbalance, protecting lower population states, such as Alaska, Delaware, Wyoming, Hawaii, Mississippi, Vermont, West Virginia, and New Mexico, from political irrelevancy compared to major population centers like New York City and Los Angeles. (*See page 59*)

Each State shall appoint, in such Manner as the Legislature thereof may direct, a Number of Electors, equal to the whole Number of Senators and Representatives to which the State may be entitled in the Congress: but no Senator or Representative, or Person holding an Office of Trust or Profit under the United States, shall be appointed an Elector.

Constitution of the United States, Article II, Section 1.

PROLOGUE
The Electoral College Is No Accident

After the 2016 presidential election some Americans objected to the existence of an old American institution, the Electoral College. That's because one candidate, Democrat Hillary Clinton, lost the election even though she won the popular vote. People object on the grounds that the Electoral College is "undemocratic" and claim that the College is merely a historical accident into which the country's founders stumbled.

This view is demonstrably flawed and reflects a woeful lack of any true understanding of the critical interlocking design of the Constitution and its intended purpose.

Objections to the Electoral College and broader complaints about the Constitution are virtually all rooted in the assumption that unfettered "democracy" is the only ideal which should characterize all major governing principles. The founders believed in consent of the governed. But they were also well aware that unfettered democracy was and is a substantial, potentially lethal, threat to freedom and individual liberty. Our founders supported institutions such as states, which check the federal government, and representative bodies, which check popular passion, in order to protect against majoritarian abuses. The founders were deeply concerned that a pure democracy might bring to power a demagogue who in turn would take the country down the road to tyranny. A demagogue might be able to manipulate the opinions and attitudes in major population centers so that those centers swamp the more diversified interests of the country at large.

The old cliché is "one man, one vote, one time." That is, voters enraptured with a demagogue will vote the demagogue in, only to find themselves losing their right to vote freely under the demagogue. The current chaos in that formerly wealthy country of Venezuela provides an overwhelming example of the devastating impact that a powerful, popularly elected, centralized government can create. What is incredible is that Venezuela's move from civilization and wealth to chaos and poverty took only fifteen years.

The founders were well aware of such risk and designed an ingenious system to protect the individual citizen from the potential crushing power of an oppressive national government. They crafted a combination of democracy, direct government, and republic, representative government. The legislative branch, the House of Representatives, whose membership is apportioned by population, reflects our democratic nature. The Senate, whose members were originally chosen by state legislatures, reflected the "republic" in our national identity.

Thomas Jefferson said: "The natural progress of things is for the government to gain ground and for liberty to yield." Over two and a half centuries since the nation's founding, Jefferson proves correct. The power of the national government has indeed gained ground, as exemplified by the change in the senatorial election process accomplished by the ratification of the Seventeenth Amendment in 1913. The Amendment provided for direct popular election of senators, rather than election by their respective state legislatures. Both houses of Congress are now chosen directly by the voters. Untethered from state governments, senators became quasi-national figures. The change significantly reduced individual state's influence on their senators' activities. This was a far more profound alteration in the nation's power structure than is commonly understood. Elimination of the Electoral College would be an even more radical, and more dangerous, shift toward that unfettered democracy.

While critics of the Electoral College complain that the College somehow favors low-population states to the detriment of high-population states, in reality the College's purpose is to protect the low-population states from the potential tyranny of the mob. That is why the College was such an essential component of the agreement among the states to form a union. There is simply no way the smaller states would have given up any sovereignty to a federal government without some protection from domination by the large states. Far from being an antiquated accident of history, the Electoral College is an integral, necessary component of a well-thought-through interlocking system which has as its primary goal protection of freedom and individual liberty.

The purpose of this publication is to provide a clear and concise explanation of the history and purpose of the Electoral College. Results such as the 2016 election were clearly anticipated, not accidents to be avoided. The United States was created as a representative republic, not a pure democracy.

Our founders demonstrated a prescient, awesome understanding of human nature. They designed a system of government which preserves order while at the same time protecting individual liberty.

As readers know, capturing the subtle function of the Electoral College is not an easy task. Yet author Josiah Peterson of The King's College has managed that feat. The quality of this book reflects the quality of King's, where Mr. Peterson teaches and which he attended as an undergraduate. Both King's President Gregory Thornbury and I are grateful to Mr. Peterson, who embodies the possibilities that King's offers.

Thomas H. Patrick

INTRODUCTION

I magine a presidential Election Night.

The television announcer appears on the screen. Beside the announcer is the familiar map of the United States. But inside the outline, there are no states. There is just a running vote total for the candidates that managed to garner the most favorable national name recognition. There are celebrity candidates like Mark Zuckerberg, Howard Schultz, Kanye West, and Oprah Winfrey, billionaires like Michael Bloomberg and Tom Steyer, and perhaps a couple of candidates pushed hard by powerful lobbies such as the American Association of Retired Persons (AARP) or the National Rifle Association (NRA). All these are candidates you've seen plenty of times on television, but who have never visited your home state. And all are vying for top billing in a national popularity contest.

We don't expect an Election Night tally to look like that. But that is how a presidential Election Night would look without one of the institutions constructed by America's founders: the Electoral College. The College is the formal body of electors whose votes actually determine the next president of the United States.

In the Electoral College, states matter. State-based electors, selected through statewide or district based polls, are the real determiners of the U.S. presidential election. 538 electors gather in their respective state capitals about a month after the election and cast their ballots to determine the next president of the United States. Nearly every state in America employs a winner-take-all system, assigning every elector in their state to represent the candidate who polled best in the state.

Sometimes the national popular vote doesn't align with the Electoral College's outcome. This happened in 2016 when Hillary Clinton led Donald Trump by over 2.8 million votes. Yet Donald Trump secured the Electoral College by 304 to 227 votes. Many Americans—from congressmen to comedians, college students, to professional commentators—say the system isn't fair. Angry voters declare the Electoral College unworthy of our democratic ideals, tilted right and, above all, outdated. Some even charge that the Electoral College is racist.

"Why should these electors outweigh the will of millions of voters?" they ask. Five times in history, the popular vote and the electoral vote have conflicted, the critics note—and that is enough.

But the critics are wrong.

As this book will show, the Electoral College, and the 2016 election, were no accidents. Our founders didn't err when they created the Electoral College. They knew situations like 2016 could happen. A major benefit of the Electoral College is the protection of individual states from domination by large population centers, and it did precisely that in 2016. That was part of the plan. The founders created the College for reasons that made sense then and still make sense today.

The primary goal of the founders was to sustain our national balance between two forms of government: republican, or representative, on the one hand and democratic, with the people directly voting on candidates and issues, on the other. Deliberative representative institutions check the impulses of majorities that might undermine the freedoms a republic aims to protect. Almost all European populations vote indirectly for their heads of government—usually prime ministers rather than presidents—by way of their parliaments. In countries that choose their chief executive by direct vote, it's not uncommon for the original, democratically elected, president to accumulate more and more power and bring about the effectual end of that democracy. Venezuela's Hugo Chávez gets mention in the prologue to this book and provides a stark example of how the problems created by an elected dictator can live on after the original dictator has died through the political machinery he created. But France's Louis Napoleon, Argentina's Juan Peron, Egypt's Mohamed Morsi, the Philippines' Ferdinand Marcos, Zimbabwe's Robert Mugabe, and the Democratic Republic of the Congo's Joseph Kabila represent further sad evidence of the results of democratic programs going awry. Think of Turkey, where President Recep Tayyip Erdogan recently changed the law to give himself more power. Once a demagogue wins, he aggregates power; and after a time under the demagogue, voters find their voice is no longer heard.

To preserve republican government, the founders placed great emphasis on a second sort of balance, the balance of powers among the three branches of government: executive, judicial, and legislative. The United States differs from most European countries in not having the chief executive selected by members of the legislature. Our founders observed the legislative tyrannies of England and the Netherlands and did not want to create that kind of system in America. The founders decided that while an intermediary ought to be involved in electing the president, that intermediary should not come from preexisting political classes.

The Electoral College also preserves an additional, vital, division of powers in America: the balance between the federal government and the states. Recognition of the importance of states to the American system of government spans political and partisan ideologies. As you'll see in the next chapter, James Madison and Alexander Hamilton, normally political opposites, came together on the importance of states. Even the unrivaled national centralizer, Franklin Delano Roosevelt recognized the beauty of the constitutional system in this matter, saying of the founding:

> Fortunately for the stability of our Nation, it was already apparent that the vastness of the territory presented geographical and climatic differences which gave to the States wide differences in the nature of their industry, their agriculture and their commerce…Thus, it was clear to the framers of our Constitution that the greatest possible liberty of self-government must be given to each State, and that any national administration attempting to make all laws for the whole Nation, such as was wholly practical in Great Britain, would inevitably

result at some future time in a dissolution of the Union itself. The preservation of this "Home Rule" by the States is not a cry of jealous Commonwealths seeking their own aggrandizement at the expense of sister States. It is a fundamental necessity if we are to remain a united country.

If states are to be able to provide for their own unique needs, they must have some voice in selecting the national leaders or risk having their needs subsumed by a narrowly partisan national agenda.

The founders set the number of each state's electors at the sum of their senators (always two) and representatives (based on population as determined by the decennial census) in Congress. Even remote or low population states get two senators. Since we have 50 states now and the District of Columbia was granted the same electors as the lowest population state, there are a total of 538 electors who vote for president. This means it takes 270 electors to win a modern day election.

States may determine how their electors are chosen, and all but two have chosen a winner-take-all system. So in Michigan, for example, the candidate with the most Michigander votes gets all 16 of Michigan's Electoral College votes. What about when no candidate wins a majority in the Electoral College? Or what

MYTH I

The Electoral College was an accident, an unprincipled compromise made by the Constitution's Framers.

In fact, the Electoral College was a necessary and ingenious compromise allowing states to preserve their power while signing onto a national constitution. Far from unprincipled, the Electoral College promotes the division of power among the branches of government and among the various levels of government: national, state, and local.

about when the Electoral College vote results in a tie? Then, the founders said, the contest goes to the House of Representatives: "the House of Representatives shall immediately choose by Ballot one of them [the candidates] for President." (Art. II sec. 2). In this ballot each state would get just one vote.

The result is that outcomes under the Electoral College are sometimes different than they would be if we elected presidents by a national popular vote. If the election were determined based on the popular vote alone, then a candidate could win with an overwhelming majority in a couple of very populous states (say, California and New York) lose every other state by significant margins, and still win the election. The Electoral College requires a candidate to win at least 11 states to secure a victory. Since it is unlikely that all 11 of the largest states—California, Texas, New York, Florida, Illinois, Pennsylvania, Ohio, Michigan, Georgia, North Carolina, and New Jersey—will vote the same way, candidates must compete in other states to be sure they exceed the 270 threshold. This has meant the candidate that wins the most states almost always wins the election.

This representation of the states in the process is important. States have their own identities and governments, the differences between which to this day allow us a kind of natural experiment in governance. And yet without the Electoral College, the TV commentators truly would not call states' results, but rather call the results for factions: "and the elderly vote seems to be going to…."

In addition to highlighting the founders' vision for the country, this book will show how the Electoral College system played out in the presidential elections of two ideologically polar candidates: John Quincy Adams and Andrew Jackson. The stunning election of Abraham Lincoln and other case studies will show how the Electoral College can be a vehicle for third parties and reformers by lowering the threshold for them to gain political significance. You'll also see that far from cementing a few swing states as the country's kingmakers, the Electoral College ensures that every state has the chance to be significant. With this context in place, the book will conclude with the 21st century elections and the future of the Electoral College.

The 2016 presidential election was not a fluke. All of Hillary Clinton's popular vote lead could be attributed to New York City and Los Angeles—just six counties out of 3,007 nationwide. Our founders didn't want the country to be controlled solely by the major population centers. No state would have signed on to an agreement that all but ensured their political impotence. While a popular vote system would remove the influence of swing states it would replace them with swing cities. A demagogue could rally a couple major population centers and win the election while earning meager support throughout the rest of the country. Such a system would also favor wild political movements or demagogic celebrities, even more than our current system. As "the representative of the people," a politician elected by such a system could claim a mandate to resist the moderating influences of states and divisions of government. In other words, the popular vote could be a mandate for dictatorship.

Changing from the Electoral College to a popular vote system wouldn't have guaranteed Hillary Clinton the election in 2016. For starters, both major candidates would have campaigned differently. Clinton had 2.8 million more votes than Trump, but she had only a plurality, not a popular majority. She actually garnered a smaller percentage of the popular vote than Al Gore in 2000, who also lacked an absolute popular majority (over 50 percent of the popular vote). Her loss came not because the Electoral College was rigged against her. Clinton lost because she did what no candidate in an Electoral College system can afford to do: she ignored the interests of too many non-coastal states.

From the original intent of the founders to the vehicle for reform to the dynamic competition among the states, the Electoral College preserves a division of government that protects the interests of all Americans. The College serves at once as a buffer and a political mirror: a check, though not checkmate, on too-rapid political change and a facilitator of necessary shifts in established party platforms. Far from an accident or an injustice, the Electoral College is critical to our republic.

CHAPTER 1
"A Republic, If You Can Keep It"

When the Framers of what became the United States Constitution met in Philadelphia over the summer of 1787, they faced the challenge of creating a form of government that was acceptable to the thirteen states while upholding republican principles. The Framers were well aware that their project—forming a new government by deliberation rather than conquest—was unprecedented. Almost every detail of the new government was hotly debated by the brightest minds of the period. Benjamin Franklin is said to have succinctly summed up the Framers' hopes in response to a woman asking him what sort of government the country would have: "A Republic, if you can keep it." The Electoral College is one of their most ingenious creations for preserving the republic, generating buy-in from the states while preserving the principles of self-government for which they had so recently fought.

A republican government, rare and usually short lived by historical standards (the failure of the English and Dutch republics, as well as that of Greece and Rome, certainly weighed on the founders' minds), rests on the consent of the governed, with representatives creating laws through deliberation that are enforced through due process. That was the Framers' standard. Creating a system that best approximates this standard, taking into account human nature marked by selfishness and ambition, was their project.

Having established a bicameral, or two-house, legislature to create laws, James Madison, the primary author of the Constitution, initially proposed that the convention adopt a legislative model for selecting the president. Members of congress would vote for the chief executive, similar to how European parliaments elect their prime ministers. The legislative model was part of Madison's so called "Virginia Plan," which served as the starting point for deliberation. Madison's proposal had the advantage of ensuring a united government in which the executive and the legislature would likely operate from the same agenda.

The convention delegates were skeptical of Madison's parliamentary plan. They were concerned that it would make the chief executive too dependent on the legislature, especially if the executive was hoping for reelection. (The Twenty-second Amendment, limiting presidents to two terms, wouldn't become law until 1951.) They found the legislative branch, the branch responsible for passing laws, already the most powerful. They knew enough history and had their own experience to tell them power corrupts. Corrupt lawmakers would no longer make laws on the basis of public interest but rather in the interest of preserving their own power, and the republican foundation of government would be lost. Thus republican principles required a separation of powers between the executive and legislative branches, such that each branch could check and balance the other.

In order to keep the president from becoming dependent on the will of Congress, it was important that executive power, the power to enforce laws, be vested in an office separate from direct legislative influence. General George Washington, a Virginian himself and president of the Constitutional Convention, broke with his fellow Virginians to vote against the plan of having the chief executive chosen by the legislature.

Pennsylvania delegate James Wilson proposed a plan to select the president through a national popular vote, similar to what many agitate for today. Electing the president on the basis of direct votes by the people

MYTH II

The Electoral College violates the democratic principles of the founders.

The founders were skeptical of direct democracy, fearing manipulative demagogues and oppressive majorities. They preferred the model of a republic, founded on the rule of the law, governed by deliberating representatives responsive to and resting on the consent of the governed. While respecting the interests of the majority and allowing some populism, the Electoral College protects against the abuses of democratic majorities when they might infringe on individual rights and deliberative government.

would certainly separate the executive power from the legislative. This was democracy, in contrast to a republic. But convention delegates saw that this plan, too, had flaws. The delegates feared a sudden craze for a charismatic figure might power him into the presidency and set the stage for autocracy. John Witherspoon, a pastor and president of Princeton, wrote, "Pure democracy cannot subsist long nor be carried far into the departments of state—it is very subject to caprice and the madness of popular rage." Noah Webster, of *Webster's Dictionary* fame, observed that democracy "is often the most tyrannical government on earth." The Constitution's Framers knew that while history was filled with examples of democracies turned tyrannies—see Greek city states and Rome—there were no long-lasting examples of free republics. They didn't want a system that would enable a popularly elected tyrant.

Additionally, the Framers were concerned that the average voter would not be able to determine the proper qualifications for president, or be able to thoroughly evaluate the candidates. How could a farmer in Georgia determine whether a governor from New Hampshire was qualified to serve as president in a time of trade wars with Europe and attacks from Barbary pirates? Even today with modern communication, it is difficult for citizens to be thoroughly and adequately informed about the history and temperament of political candidates. Ultimately, James Wilson's national vote proposal was rejected by a 9 - 2 vote of the states.

If the legislature is unable to select the president because of the division of powers, and if the people ought not determine who should lead them, what alternative could be found? Oliver Ellsworth, a Connecticut lawyer who later became a Senator and Supreme Court Justice, proposed a plan by which the people would be involved in selecting the chief executive by means of choosing electors who would then choose the president on their behalf. Importantly, these electors were not allowed to be current members of Congress or other nationally elected office-holders. While voters couldn't be expected to spend all their time vetting presidential candidates, they could be expected to select representatives on their behalf to do so. This new plan gained wide support.

Alexander Hamilton, focusing primarily on the independence of the electors from the whims of popular sentiment, defended the proposal in Federalist 68, writing thus:

> The process of election affords a moral certainty, that the office of President will never fall to the lot of any man who is not in an eminent degree endowed with the requisite qualifications. Talents for low intrigue, and

the little arts of popularity, may alone suffice to elevate a man to the first honors in a single State; but it will require other talents, and a different kind of merit, to establish him in the esteem and confidence of the whole Union, or of so considerable a portion of it as would be necessary to make him a successful candidate for the distinguished office of President of the United States.

Since the creation of the Constitution, most states have opted to use their authority to set their own election laws to bind their entire slate of electors to the popular vote outcome of their state. This is quite contrary to the founders' original imagining of the institution, whereby electors would be elected from various districts and be free to vote for whom they saw fit. This means electors are not so independent today as Hamilton, and other founders, hoped and demagoguery is therefore less restrained than it might be.

How were the numbers of electors per state to be determined? This matter had already been effectively settled by an earlier debate at the Constitutional Convention. When determining how many legislators each state should have in the national legislature, the small state of New Jersey proposed every state have an equal number of legislators. Delegates from the large state of Virginia proposed states be allocated legislators proportional

MYTH III

The Electoral College is racist.

The existence and continuation of slavery is the greatest mar on the American founding. It couldn't help but pervert everything it touched.

But many of our founders, including those that drafted and promoted the Electoral College, opposed slavery. The father of the College, Oliver Ellsworth, even called upon the convention twice to abolish slavery.

The "Three-Fifths Clause," whereby slaves were counted as 3/5th of a person for congressional apportionment, is widely reviled. That is because people believe that by counting slaves at 3/5th each, Framers were trying to dehumanize African Americans. But actually the clause was a compromise forced by abolitionist states in the name of reducing slave state representation. The pro-slavery regimes of the Southern states wanted each slave to be counted as "one" or five-fifths, so that those states would have more congressional seats. Most Northern abolitionists wanted the slaves not to be counted at all, in order to weaken the representation of the slave state governments. The Three-Fifths Clause was actually a compromise forced on the South by Northern states.

As you will see in Chapter III, the Electoral College also became the vehicle by which Abraham Lincoln was elected, bringing about the end of slavery and the Three-Fifths Clause, and the distortions created in congressional and electoral apportionment.

to their populations. This early and fierce division posed both practical and principled challenges. How could all states agree on a single plan that seemed to favor the interests of some states over others? What would low-population states gain from yielding their sovereignty to a national government in which more populous states would control the lawmaking power? If the new government were to maintain any semblance of federalism, lower-population states would have to be given a larger voice.

A move known as the Connecticut Compromise broke the stalemate. The government's two legislative bodies would reflect both principles. It would have a larger House of Representatives whose makeup is based on population, and a smaller Senate in which each state has two Senators. This "Great Compromise" secured power for the American states and also created a new check on legislative power, by dividing the legislative branch in two.

James Madison, who had initially proposed a parliamentary system for electing the president before considering a popular vote system, saw the prudence of electing the president along the same lines as the Connecticut Compromise. In Federalist 39, written to argue for the ratification of the U.S. Constitution, Madison wrote:

The House of Representatives will derive its powers from the people of America… So far the government is NATIONAL, not FEDERAL. The Senate, on the other hand, will derive its powers from the States, as political and coequal societies; and these will be represented on the principle of equality in the Senate… So far the government is FEDERAL, not NATIONAL. The executive power will be derived from a very compound source. The immediate election of the President is to be made by the States in their political characters. The votes allotted to them are in a compound ratio, which considers them partly as distinct and coequal societies, partly as unequal members of the same society … From this aspect of the government it appears to be of a mixed character, presenting at least as many FEDERAL as NATIONAL features.

The Framers, following Madison's new recommendation, decided to adopt the same approach to apportioning electors among the states, giving more weight to large states while ensuring that each state has a meaningful voice. Each state would have a number of electors equal to the number of its representatives in the House, plus the two from the Senate. The Framers wanted to be sure, however, that the legislators didn't find a way to game the system so they added a provision that no sitting federal government official could serve as an elector.

This plan met broad approval, and the final language on the selection of our chief executive can be found in Article II Section 1 of the United States Constitution:

> Each State shall appoint, in such Manner as the Legislature thereof may direct, a Number of Electors, equal to the whole Number of Senators and Representatives to which the State may be entitled in the Congress: but no Senator or Representative, or Person holding an Office of Trust or Profit under the United States, shall be appointed an Elector.

The Electoral College was forged in compromise, but that compromise upheld important republican principles of self-government and the rule of law. The system is an ingenious innovation, not outdated, and it is a critical key to keeping our republic.

CHAPTER 2

The First Assault on the Electoral College – And the College's Victory

The Electoral College faced its first test early on. Those who call the Electoral College "undemocratic" today may be surprised to find they have an early ally: the dueling, Indian-killing, Wall Street hating seventh President of the United States, Andrew Jackson. "Old Hickory" disliked the Electoral College because of his strong faith in popular democracy. The people should rule, Jackson thought. But a personal motivation also drove him: revenge. He believed he was the one who ought to rule for the people and, in a previous election, the Electoral College and the son of a former president— John Quincy Adams—had got in his way. In 1824, Jackson became the first man to lose a presidential election while winning a plurality of the popular vote.

The details of the 1824 contest bear some resemblance to modern elections. John Quincy Adams belonged to the closest thing America had at that time to a political dynasty. His father, John Adams, had been a respected founder and the second president of the United States. From birth, John Quincy Adams had been groomed to lead. His father had taken him as a child on European diplomatic missions. The ambitious Adams scion became Ambassador to the Netherlands by age 26, Ambassador to Prussia at 29, U.S. Senator and Harvard professor at 35, Ambassador to Russia and then England in his 40s, and the nation's eighth Secretary of State at 50.

The younger Adams, a student of history and politics, recognized that "[t]he experience of all former ages had shown that of all human governments, democracy was the most unstable, fluctuating and short lived." That's not to say he didn't respect the will of the people. But he respected it so much that he wasn't willing to let fits of passion overwhelm the country's commitment to rule of law and human rights. Adams didn't want a democratically elected dictator.

Adams' opponent, by contrast, was a populist's populist. Though born only a few months earlier than John Quincy Adams, Andrew Jackson had lived a very different life. Jackson never knew his father, who died shortly before Jackson was born. During his teenage years, Jackson served as a courier for the Carolina militia fighting in the Revolutionary War, and was captured by the British. Jackson's mother died shortly after his release, leaving him an orphan at age 14. A man of incredible grit and determination, Jackson taught himself law, and eventually saw success as a country lawyer and early real-estate investor in what became the state of Tennessee. Later, Jackson briefly served as a Congressman, U.S. Senator, and Tennessee Supreme Court Judge. His private businesses also flourished. Jackson at first bought a small cotton farm and later acquired more than 1,000 acres in a cotton plantation. Jackson's real claim to fame came as a military commander, serving as a Colonel and later Major General over the Tennessee militia during the War of 1812 and the First Seminole War. After his military victories, he governed New Orleans under martial law and later served as Military Governor of Florida under President James Monroe.

While there were several formidable candidates in the 1824 election, the real race came down to America's diplomat, Adams, and America's favorite general, Jackson. Adams gathered about 31 percent of the votes, winning big in the electorally rich

The Twelfth Amendment

In the original creation of the Electoral College, presidential electors each cast two votes for president and the candidate who received the second highest number of electoral votes became vice president. In the election of 1800, a majority of electors aligned with the Democratic Republican Party (no longer in existence). They wanted to elect Thomas Jefferson president and Aaron Burr vice president, but the elector who was supposed to abstain from voting for Burr (giving Jefferson a one-vote lead) forgot, thus resulting in a tie and sending the election to the House of Representatives for the first "contingent election." After the House, under the influence of Alexander Hamilton, gave the presidency to Jefferson, the new president quickly proposed an amendment to the constitution by which electors would cast two separate votes, one for president and one for vice president, to prevent such a scenario from happening again. To date, the Twelfth Amendment is the fastest amendment to go from proposal to ratification, in just over six months, and it has helped ensure that presidents and vice presidents are on the same team.

Northeast, but only collecting three additional electors from outside the region, from Louisiana (where not all recalled Jackson's rule favorably) and Illinois. Jackson, on the other hand, won close to 41.5 percent of the votes, picking up states from Pennsylvania to Mississippi to Illinois and even one elector from New York. Adams claimed 84 electors to Jackson's 99, but 78 electors had divided themselves among the other "also ran" candidates, preventing either Jackson or Adams from obtaining an absolute electoral majority required to become president.

This threw the election into the House of Representatives for the country's second "contingent election," as such House votes are known, the first having been the election of 1800. Even contingent elections ensure that states matter, as Representatives vote by state, with one vote per state. Thirteen of 24 state delegations in the House handed the presidency to John Quincy Adams. That made Adams the first—but not the last—president to win the election despite another candidate securing a plurality of the popular vote. A majority of states thought Adams was the safer choice for the country, and they made him president.

Jackson claimed Adams had made "a corrupt bargain" with House Speaker Henry Clay, who conveniently was given control of the State

Department in the Adams administration. Jackson and his political ally Martin Van Buren, the United States Senator from New York, began the formation of a new political party, the antecedent to the modern Democrats. Meanwhile Adams' supporters contrived to form the short-lived "National Republican" party that would soon turn into the Whig Party.

Adams' presidency was not especially eventful, in part because Adams respected the limits of the executive office and declined to try to out-maneuver a Congress characterized by bitter partisanship. Adams advocated the development of national infrastructure and nonintervention in foreign affairs, and sought to protect the rights of Native Americans on the frontier. His most controversial measures were a tariff to protect domestic industry and his support for the National Bank, something like the Federal Reserve of today.

In 1828, the people were ready for a rematch. Andrew Jackson cleared the field of third-party candidates and rallied support against Adams' tariff and the central bank. As a result, Jackson went on to capture a majority of states and with them, the election. This time Jackson took both the popular vote and the Electoral College, the latter by a comfortable 178-83 margin.

Though Jackson had deplored the Electoral College before, now he enjoyed the authority his turnout there gave him. In any case Jackson saw his role not as a steward of the country and the country's laws, but rather as the embodiment of the sovereign "will of the people."

His Inaugural address made that clear:

> To be elected … to administer the affairs of a government deriving all its powers from the will of the people, a government whose vital principle is the right of the people to control its measures, and whose only object and glory are the equal happiness and freedom of all the members of the confederacy, cannot but penetrate me with the most powerful and mingled emotions of thanks, on the one hand, for the honor conferred on me, and on the other, of solemn apprehensions for the safety of the great and important interests committed to my charge.

Jackson's first order of business in his first address to Congress? Telling lawmakers it was time to do away with the Electoral College. It was immoral, he said, to thwart the will of the majority. His "democratic" language diverged from the republican verbiage adopted by the Framers of the Constitution. "To the people belongs the right of electing their Chief magistrate," he said. "[I]t was never designed that their choice should in any case be defeated." Jackson recommended an amendment to the Constitution to "remove intermediate agency in the election of the President and vice President." Foreshadowing modern critics, Jackson saw the Constitution as an "experiment" open to "remedy," rather than a system designed to check and balance power such as his.

Jackson's alternative was to let the people choose the president directly. If no candidate received an absolute majority, Jackson posited, there would have to be a runoff election between the top two vote winners. Such a system might have stymied the elections of almost a third of our presidents who won without absolute majorities. That group includes candidates such as James Polk, Zachary Taylor, James Buchanan, Abraham Lincoln, James Garfield, Grover Cleveland (twice), Woodrow Wilson (twice), Harry Truman, John F. Kennedy, Richard Nixon, and Bill Clinton (also twice), not to mention popular vote runners up, Rutherford Hayes, Benhamin Harrison, George W. Bush, and Donald Trump.

Over Jackson's eight years in office, he defined the active presidency, vetoing more laws than any president preceding him and any succeeding him until after the Civil War. Jackson was the original populist. His rags-to-riches and war-hero status won him the hearts of the American people. He fought for many noble causes, including the expansion of suffrage to more classes of people. But ultimately he was motivated by his belief that he himself was the voice of the people. If the people wanted slaves and Indian removal—or if Jackson thought that's what the people wanted—he gave it to them.

But his efforts to abolish the Electoral College proved unsuccessful. While Jackson may have erroneously considered the Electoral College to be a regrettable compromise on the part of the founders, voters and legislators still appreciated the purposeful design of the institution as a check against mob rule. So Congress was reluctant to remove this check on the forceful Jackson.

The observant Alexis de Tocqueville considered Jackson a dangerous demagogue: "General Jackson stoops to gain the favor of the majority; but when he feels that his popularity is secure, he overthrows all obstacles in the pursuit of the objects which the community approves or of those which it does not regard with jealousy." Tocqueville noted that Jackson was also vindictive: "Supported by a power that his predecessors never had, he tramples on his personal enemies, whenever they cross his path, with a facility without example; he takes upon himself the responsibility of measures that no one before him would have ventured to attempt. He even treats the national representatives with a disdain approaching to insult."

"He is a favorite who sometimes treats his master roughly," Tocqueville concluded.

The Jackson presidency lasted eight years but his populist spirit never fully died. Yet the Electoral College endures, buoyed by the belief in a more deliberative selection of the president. The Democrats that emerged post-Jackson moved into the mainstream: Martin Van Buren, Jackson's successor, proved more organizer than firebrand. And soon the Democrats would be overwhelmed by the populist "log cabin and hard cider" campaign of the Whig war-hero, William Henry Harrison. The Democrats came back with sober Senator James K. Polk for a term before the Whigs got their last man in the White House, former General Zachary Taylor. During that stretch of American history, the College served different roles: crystallizing discontent with the status quo, but also checking change when it came too rapidly. The Whigs tired of having to run reckless, one-term, war heroes, and knew their party was on the decline. The Electoral College was crucial in helping to facilitate needed reforms—but that's for the next chapter.

CHAPTER 3
The Hope for Third Parties and Reformers

Without the Electoral College, third parties and reformers (barring celebrities or self-funded billionaires) wouldn't stand a chance. The abolition of the College would lead to the concentration of political power in wealthy elites and a two-party system. One of the most dramatic examples is provided by that underdog reform candidate, Abraham Lincoln.

Many people know Lincoln as the man who led the North to victory in the Civil War, and brought about the end of slavery. Lincoln is a hero, honored with a monument in Washington D.C. His profile graces both the penny and the five-dollar bill. Fewer people realize that Lincoln was an upstart candidate running on the ticket of a relatively new political party against well-established political figures.

Lincoln, a self-taught lawyer from backwoods Illinois, had served in Congress for two years during the 1840s and retired to go home and practice law. He joined a brand new political party, the Republicans, united by a single issue: curtailing slavery. He was running in a four-way race against the sitting Vice President, John C. Breckinridge, who was a pro-slavery Democrat with an impressive resume as two-term Senator and former Secretary of War. Another opponent boasted equally formidable credentials: John Bell, running for the Constitutional Union Party, who had served as Speaker of the House. Also in the contest was the man who'd defeated Lincoln in his run for U.S. Senate in 1856: Stephen Douglas, a Northern Democrat. Lincoln had a much lower national profile to start out. He was lucky to even win the Republican nomination over New York's U.S. Senator, William Seward.

Lincoln's success is all the more surprising considering that his party had existed for barely six years. The Republican Party was founded in 1854 primarily to oppose the Kansas-Nebraska Act, which allowed the expansion of slavery into the U.S. territories. The new party garnered support from abolitionists, the remnants of Martin Van Buren's failed "Free Soil" Party, the anti-slavery faction of the briefly-lived "Know-Nothing" Party, former members of

The 1856 Election Results

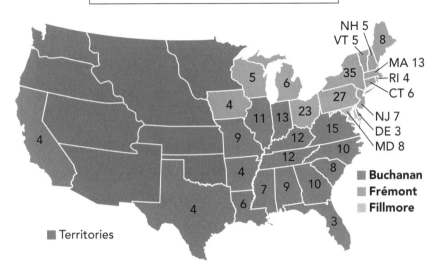

the defunct Whig Party, and even some conscientious northern Democrats. With concentrated pockets of support, Republicans managed to win 13 House seats in the 1854 midterm elections. The following year they won three northern state governorships.

So how did Lincoln become president? In 1856, the Republican Party managed to get its candidate, California Senator John C. Fremont, on the ballot in 18 out of 31 states, failing to make the ballot in 13 southern slave states. Still, the Republican Party was in the running for 187 electoral votes, with only 149 needed to win. The Republicans won low population states with pluralities, but under the winner-take-all system, their party collected all the electoral votes of those states. In what was the final nail in the coffin for the Whig Party, Fremont bested the former Whig President, Millard Fillmore, for the second place finish behind the ultimate victor, Democrat James Buchanan. The Republican Party won almost one-third of the popular vote, but took almost 40 percent of the electors by winning eleven of eighteen states where it was on the ballot. Only with the Electoral College could a new party gain traction so quickly, being able to focus on areas where it already had existing strength.

After the 1856 election, the Republican Party was able to translate its strong finish into greater national support. Lincoln built on Fremont's foundation, getting on the ballot in four additional states, giving him access to 230 out of the 304 Electoral College votes with only 153 required to win. And win he did, with 180 electoral votes and 18 states, from the North, Midwest, and West. Despite this resounding victory in the Electoral College, Abraham Lincoln won the presidency with only 1.87 million of the 4.69 million votes cast, less than 40 percent of the popular vote. He took California with less than 33 percent of the vote. But the three other candidates combined could not beat him in the Electoral College. The winner-take-all and state-based system of the Electoral College gave triumph

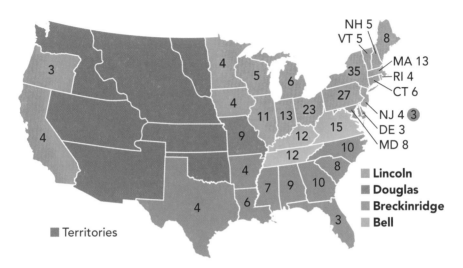

to a new man with a new agenda. Had there been a popular vote system sending Lincoln into a runoff, the pro-slavery forces would likely have consolidated around Lincoln's opponent and our nation's history with slavery might have lasted even longer.

Lincoln's election was far from democratically majoritarian. He ran his campaign on the single issue of fulfilling the Declaration's promise of "All men are created equal." He didn't believe in "majoritarianism," simply letting the majority run roughshod over minority rights. Lincoln vehemently opposed Stephen Douglas's platform of "popular sovereignty," in which anything the people want and vote for is legitimate. Lincoln believed that governing legitimacy is derived from the consent of the governed because the governed have inherent human dignity and the right to self-government. Laws that undermine human dignity and self-government undermine the very foundation upon which the rule of law and legitimate governing authority rest.

Of course it's no one's ideal to have presidents elected by small pluralities, even when they do win a majority of states. The states who lost the election were swift to announce that Lincoln was in effect "not our president" and promptly seceded from the Union. They refused to recognize what the Electoral College told them, that Lincoln was the candidate that appealed to a majority of people in a majority of states, and insisted that their popular sovereignty must be respected. They rejected the rule of law and the principles of self-government that Lincoln recognized and the Electoral College affirms.

The remarkable victory of Abraham Lincoln and the Republican Party is hardly the typical example of new party campaigns. But history has also demonstrated third parties have used the Electoral College to gain traction that they never could achieve in a national popular vote, even when they don't win the presidency.

One example occurred during the election of 1892. Citizens in Western and Plains states worried that the Eastern states were adopting tariffs and monetary policies that hurt their agricultural interests. The newly formed Populist Party nominated Iowa Representative and former "Greenback Party" candidate James Weaver for president. That nomination secured Weaver ballot access in a sizable majority of states. Weaver didn't have nearly the name recognition or support to overcome the two former presidents he was running against. (Former President Grover Cleveland would successfully challenge sitting President Benjamin Harrison to take his seat back, making Cleveland the only president to serve two non-consecutive terms.) But Weaver did manage to win almost 8.5 percent of the popular vote, 5 states, and 22 electors.

One might be tempted to call Weaver's candidacy a failure, a populist defeated by big-money establishment politicians. But that would take a myopic view of history. The real legacy of Weaver's candidacy and the Populist Party efforts can be seen in the way they shaped political parties and platforms going forward. By winning several states and taking electoral votes away from his challengers, Weaver called notice to the harms of tariffs and Eastern monetary policy. No future candidate could afford to ignore the demand for tariff relief.

By 1896, therefore, at least one party had learned the importance of rural voters. Democrats nominated as their candidate William Jennings Bryan, a pro-

MYTH IV

The Electoral College always favors conservatives.

It's true the Electoral College has most recently helped Donald Trump and George W. Bush, two Republicans, win the White House without popular majorities. But in the past this same institution has also helped Democrats without popular majorities win the presidency and govern with political legitimacy. Of the 19 elections won without popular majorities, ten were won by Democrats, seven by Republicans, one by a Whig and one by a Democratic Republican. These presidents include Bill Clinton, John F. Kennedy, Harry Truman, Woodrow Wilson, Abraham Lincoln, and John Quincy Adams.

regulation, anti-gold standard, anti-tariff Senator from Nebraska. "You shall not crucify mankind upon a cross of gold!" Bryan thundered. Democrats, shaken by Weaver's relative success, shifted so much between 1892 and 1896, abandoning Grover Cleveland's "sound-money," small government conservatism, that the Populist Party happily endorsed the Democrats' 1896 plateform and threw their support behind Bryan. And while Bryan, too, was ultimately unsuccessful against William McKinley, his campaign shaped the Democrats' congressional delegation and helped pave the way for progressives such as Theodore Roosevelt and Woodrow Wilson.

Then, as now, the value of the Electoral College was clear. The College both gave reformers a stage, and forced majority parties to take them seriously. That's why third—and sometimes fourth and fifth—party candidates have won states in 11 elections and electors in 20 (see Appendix A). While we've persisted with the parties launched by Andrew Jackson (Democrat) and Abraham Lincoln (Republican), there's no question that third party campaigns have elevated issues to national attention. The campaigns of James Weaver, Socialist Eugene Debs, former President Theodore Roosevelt, Wisconsin Senator Robert La Follette, South Carolina Governor Strom Thurmond, former Cabinet member Henry Wallace, Alabama

Governor George Wallace, Illinois Congressman John Anderson, businessman Ross Perot, and consumer rights advocate Ralph Nader have all elevated their causes to the national stage. These outsider campaigns force the major party candidates to take notice or risk losing states. Bill Clinton won in the Electoral College. But would Bill Clinton have pursued a balanced budget without Ross Perot? Would Al Gore and the Democrats have become as environmentalist as they are but for Ralph Nader? With the Electoral College, even a loss can be a victory for an effective third-party or reform campaign. People who want to shake up the political establishment might start thinking about how to use the Electoral College as an ally rather than seeing it as an enemy.

CHAPTER 4
Keeping States Competitive

Opponents of the Electoral College often claim that the system of winner-take-all states disadvantages lower population states or states that lean heavily toward one party over another. If true, this would mean that only a handful of large states with close political margins, "swing states," ultimately matter. This is a serious concern, as competing for votes in the various states is one of the ways by which all states have a stake in the presidency. If certain states, or whole regions of the country, can be routinely ignored, then we could conclude the system is gravely flawed.

But that is not what happens. In fact, states and regions get remembered precisely because of the College.

Even before the United States filled out the country with states from sea to shining sea, no one region has held sufficient electoral clout to determine the outcome of an election. Lincoln's overwhelming northeastern base of support wouldn't have been sufficient had he not carried parts of the Midwest and the West Coast. John Adams' strong Northern base would have been insufficient but for the votes he received from Virginia, North Carolina, and Maryland. So while some regions may be more populous than others, and regions may tend to vote as a bloc due to shared interest, no single region of the country can hold sway over the rest, especially as the country has grown.

The Electoral College strikes the balance between respecting high population states' appropriate power and ensuring they don't entirely dominate lower population states. Under the Electoral College, high population states hold more sway than low population states, but to a lesser degree than they would under a popular vote system. This is because low population states' electoral vote totals are buoyed by having two senators, the same number as high population states.

The idea of a swing state is only really significant when electoral margins are close. So how often does the electoral margin fall within the range of a single state? On average, this happens a little less than every four elections. Sixteen out of the 58 elections (27.6

The Twenty-second Amendment

In a rare move to limit the power of the chief executive and the possibility for dictatorship, in 1951 the United States ratified the Twenty-second Amendment, limiting presidents to no more than ten years in office. This means presidents can serve for only two elected terms, with the possibility of completing up to two years of a predecessor's term who left office.

While some people might have a favorite politician they'd like to see serve longer, our nation recognized the corrupting influence of power. More than ten years in office could allow even a well-meaning president to totally reshape the American government, and potentially stack the Supreme Court (as Franklin Roosevelt attempted) and effectively remove one of the checks on executive power.

The Twenty-second Amendment was a prescient decision to avoid the possibility of dictatorship.

percent) in our history would have been decided in favor of the runner-up candidate, had that candidate won the largest state that went to the winner. If Nixon had held New York in 1960, (Republicans won it in 1948, 1952, and 1956), it might not have mattered that Kennedy won Texas. The 1876 election of Rutherford B. Hayes would have flipped for Samuel Tilden had any of Hayes' states defected to the other side. But that still means 42 out of 58 elections (72.4 percent) were won with electoral margins of victory large enough that even the largest states could not have altered the result.

Ohio is known as the bellwether state for its accuracy in predicating the outcome of presidential elections. Ohio's electors go to the winner 83.3 percent of the time (second only to New Mexico which gets its pick 88.9 percent of the time). Yet even Ohio has only been electorally determinative four times: in 1876, 1916, 2000, and 2004. Changing Florida's results would only affect 1876, 2000, and 2004. These two legendary swing states are useful in predicting national trends, but they are not themselves electorally determinative.

Critically, most states actually get the winner they want most of the time. This is how it ought to be when states come together to form a government. In fact, the average state votes for the winning candidate 69 percent of the time (see Appendix B). Only the District of Columbia gets its pick less than half of the time.

But don't states have to show less partisan loyalty in order to matter in an election? If a state is heavily in the camp for one candidate or party, other candidates won't even try for it. It's true that candidates will prioritize their time and resources on states they think they can win, but to think that states are locked in to a particular political party, as Hillary Clinton did in 2016, is to take a very myopic view of electoral history.

Take a look at this electoral map from 1900, when Republican William McKinley won the presidency. It's remarkably opposite to many recent maps. California and New York voted Republican—along with all of the Northeastern seaboard. Today the South tends to vote Republican, but in 1900 all Southern states except for West Virginia voted for Democrat William Jennings

The Election of 1900

Bryan. Democrats also won much of the Mountain West.

The 1976 Jimmy Carter/Gerald Ford showdown map features a clear East-West divide. (One Republican elector from Washington State opted to vote for up-and-coming Ronald Reagan instead of Ford.)

The Election of 1976

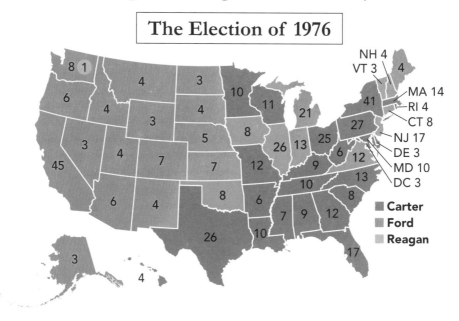

Even as recently as 1992, when Bill Clinton first ran, the U.S. map looked very different than what we'd expect to see today. The map looked like a blue and red striped flag. Democrats swept the West Coast, New Mexico up to Montana (minus Wyoming), and Louisiana up to Minnesota. The South split between Republicans and Democrats, while the Northeast took on the blue shades we've become more accustomed

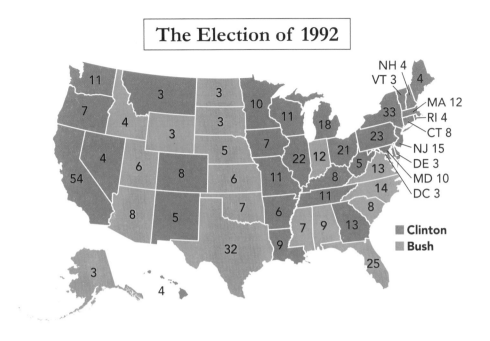

The Election of 1992

to seeing today.

As indicated by the historical maps, many states that we today consider "locked in" for one party have repeatedly shifted party allegiances. From William McKinley on, New York was Republican—but for the Great Depression—until Democrat John F. Kennedy took the state in 1960. Far from settled even then, New York chose Republican presidential candidates three more times before today.

Texas never voted Republican until it backed Dwight D. Eisenhower in the 1950s. Texans returned to the Democrats for JFK, LBJ, and even Hubert Humphrey in the 1960s, switched Republican for

Nixon's 1972 landslide, and then back to Democrats for Jimmy Carter. Ronald Reagan won the changeable Texans back to the Grand Old Party in 1982.

California is also less predictable than its reputation suggests. The Democrat incumbent Lyndon B. Johnson took the state in 1964. But otherwise, California voted consistently Republican from 1952 till 1992, and might have voted Republican even in 1992, but for independent candidate Ross Perot taking over 20 percent of the vote. Demographic shifts may make it more predictable for the foreseeable future, but history teaches us not to rest too confidently in our prophetic abilities.

The average state changes its presidential party preference every 3.81 elections, or 15.22 years, as Appendix C shows. New York, Wisconsin, Colorado, Louisiana, and Nevada, have the highest rate of party turnover. Only two states have an average length of stay with one party exceeding five election cycles: Texas and Vermont. Vermont is the most loyal state in the country, having voted Republican for 100 years straight, from 1860-1960, before giving itself to Democrats, and even then not without occasional swings. Georgia and Arkansas saw similarly long stints with the Democrats as part of the "solid South" but saw enough turnover before and after so as to make their overall averages lower.

All this means it is difficult to tell when a state will be considered a swing state and which mix of states will be necessary to win an election. It behooves a candidate not to take states for granted, as Thomas Dewey did with Ohio and California in 1948, Al Gore with West Virginia and Tennessee in 2000 and Hillary Clinton did with Wisconsin, Pennsylvania, and Michigan in 2016. And while there are large states that change their parties frequently that might accurately be called "swing states," these states rarely determine an election outcome on their own. Far from reinforcing the importance of a few states, the Electoral College makes every state important. This means individual big states, or big cities, are rarely solo kingmakers. And we can all support that result.

CHAPTER 5
The College's Continuing Purpose

The furor surrounding the Electoral College redoubled in the 2000s. That's because two presidents, George W. Bush and Donald Trump, were elected without winning even a plurality of the votes, which is to say, more than any other single candidate. These two are Republicans, but that's an accident of history. The founders did not believe that the popular vote was the most important factor, preferring a system featuring multiple contests in which candidates have to compete for and be evaluated by the electors of the several states. They didn't believe a national popularity contest would produce candidates that cared about winning support from less populous regions of the country or ensure the best evaluation of the candidates that were running.

Hillary Clinton won the popular vote by 2.8 million votes or so. She won New York City by 1.67 million votes and Los Angeles County by 1.69 million. This means that all of Hillary Clinton's popular vote lead over Trump could be attributed to just two cities. While cities matter, and will always matter, the Framers of the Constitution set up a system in which candidates have to compete in many different states, not just major population centers.

Critics of the 2016 election contend that presidents elected without a popular majority are illegitimate. Yet if this is true, then 19 out of 58 elections, almost a third of all U.S. presidential elections, are illegitimate (see Appendix E). The Electoral College boosted Woodrow Wilson with his 41.8 percent of the vote in 1912 and Abraham Lincoln with his 39.8 percent in 1860, as we've already seen. In contests where the victor didn't hold even a plurality of the popular vote— as has happened five times, including 2016—in all but one of these elections (1876), the runner-up-candidate also failed to win an absolute popular majority. Al Gore only held 48.4 percent of the popular vote to George W. Bush's 47.9 percent in 2000. Hillary Clinton had an even smaller hold with 48.2 percent of the popular vote, though Trump's total was 46.1 percent. In each case, the College favored the candidates that secured wider popularity among the states.

As recently as Bill Clinton's 1992 race, the election was won by a candidate with only 43 percent of the popular vote. The Electoral College saved Clinton from a runoff—which would be required under a principle of Jacksonian democracy—with President George H.W. Bush, which Clinton may not have won. Had this been Europe, Bush (who had 37 percent of the vote) and businessman Ross Perot (who had 19 percent) might have teamed up to create a two-party coalition government to overwhelm Clinton. And while Clinton won only five-and-a-half more percentage points than Bush, he won nearly double the electoral votes claimed by Bush. Perot won zero. Of course some Republicans were calling for the College's abolition before the next election.

It's ironic that the same rules that kept Hillary Clinton from victory secured her husband's election a quarter century before. So when asked whether or not it is wrong to deny a majority of people their preferred candidate, Americans ought to remember that a majority of people didn't actually agree on a candidate. Who's to say the 5.7 percent of people who didn't vote for Trump *or* Clinton would have preferred Clinton? Over four million people (3.27 percent of the popular vote)—an amount greater than the total difference between Hillary Clinton and Donald Trump—voted for Libertarian candidate

Gary Johnson. Almost 750,000 voters opted for the conservative independent candidate Evan McMullin. Meanwhile 1.46 million, about 1.06 percent, voted for Green Party candidate Jill Stein.

While we can't say who these voters would have selected in a runoff scenario, we can say that 30 states preferred Trump over Clinton, the same number as preferred Bush over Gore. Would it have been appropriate to let 20 states tell the other 30 what to do? Why would a state sign on to a Constitution that meant its citizens would constantly be ruled by a small group of states that happened to have a larger population at any given time? The Electoral College tends to favor the candidate who wins the most states.

If the election were determined based on the outcome of the popular vote alone, then a candidate could win 75 percent of California and New York's nearly 50 million voters, lose every other state 45-55, and still win the presidency. The Electoral College checks this problem by requiring a candidate win a minimum of 11 states (California, Texas, New York, Florida, Illinois, Pennsylvania, Ohio, Michigan, Georgia, North Carolina, and New Jersey) to win the presidency. The chances of that happening are very low, and in practice only three of 58 elections have been won by candidates with less than 50 percent of the states (1824, 1960, 1976).

MYTH V

The Electoral College unfairly favors low population states over more populous ones.

The Electoral College protects low population states from domination by high population centers.

Because electors are apportioned based on congressional representation, low population states control more electors per person than high population states.

But for the Electoral College, low population states could be completely ignored during presidential campaigns. New York City alone has a greater population than the ten smallest states combined!

All states and territories have diverse needs that ought to be considered in national elections.

Some of these territories are rural, like Alaska and Montana, while other are urban, like D.C. and Delaware. Some are homogenous, like Wyoming and Idaho while others are diverse, like Hawaii and New Mexico. Some have been trending Republican, like Mississippi and West Virginia, while others are trending Democrat, like Vermont and Rhode Island.

The Electoral College helps protect states' unique interests from being ignored by presidential candidates, ensuring all states have a voice in selecting the chief executive.

While this hypothetical may sound extreme, if the presidency were determined by national popular vote, then politicians could ignore entire swaths of the American populace, focusing on the population-rich Eastern and Western seaboards or the densely populated American cities. Rural Americans could be completely ignored by a candidate who only caters to the urban and suburban population, who together comprise almost 80 percent of the total population. Eighteen states do not have any cities with populations larger than 250,000 people: Alabama, Alaska, Arkansas, Connecticut, Delaware, Idaho, Iowa, Maine, Mississippi, Montana, New Hampshire, Rhode Island, South Carolina, South Dakota, Utah, Vermont, West Virginia, and Wyoming. What would happen to them in an election by national popular vote? According to Jishai Evers of *Dadaviz*, slightly more than 50 percent of Americans live in the country's 144 largest counties, leaving the other 49.97 percent of Americans dispersed across the 2,998 smaller counties. The two largest American counties, encompassing Los Angeles and Chicago respectively, have a combined population greater than the fourteen lowest population states combined.

It is time to step back and imagine once more what electioneering would look like under a popular vote election system. Candidates could try to form national coalitions around single galvanizing issues, like abortion or welfare reform, and disregard the myriad other interests affecting the nation. It would be easier to form majoritarian coalitions because minorities would not have as much clout on a national scale as they would in many individual states. The candidates would not have to travel much; low population states would be even less likely to receive candidate visitors. (Observers noted in the 2016 election that Trump spent more time visiting Wisconsin, Pennsylvania, Michigan, and North Carolina—states that went Democrat in 2012 but Trump in 2016—than did Hillary Clinton. He also visited New Hampshire, New Mexico, Colorado, Oregon, and Nevada, where GOP performance increased compared to 2012). Rather than trying to appeal across the aisles to compete in non-traditional territories, candidates would go to places solidly in their camp, aiming only to rally the base. Politics could become further polarized and negative as the election turned into a giant get-out-the-vote drive.

The Electoral College is a complementary and needful check on majoritarian campaigns and unrestrained executive power. It balances the popular interest with the interests of preserving a union of the various states that comprise the nation. To do away with the mildly "undemocratic" institution in selecting an executive would suggest we ought to do away with the highly undemocratic Senate, where each state receives an equal number of Senators. It's the automatic two senators that every state receives by virtue of being a state that boosts the representation for low population states in the Electoral College. If a two-vote boost in the Electoral College vote is undemocratic, how much more so a body that gives every state equal representation? Even the House, while more proportional, gives more weight to the low population state of Wyoming than its population would garner in a strictly popular contest. The Supreme Court also violates strict democratic principles, occasionally striking down laws that the majority of the people's representatives enacted. Should it, too, be done away with?

Those interested in election reform do have various constitutional options that preserve the ideals of the American political system. Arguably the most significant reform would be to switch back to an electoral system that assigned electors by congressional district, as do Maine and Nebraska today. According to Madison's notes, this is what most of the Framers had in mind and when the states began changing their systems Hamilton even proposed a constitutional amendment to require the district model.

Another area for reform is more indirect, working through the congressional apportionment system.

Currently the federal census counts non-citizen immigrants—both legal and illegal—toward the state population numbers that determine congressional apportionment. This means that states that have a high number of non-citizens, like California, Texas, New York, and Florida, are receiving additional representatives in congress, and by extension additional electors in the Electoral College, from their non-citizen residents. The states that lose influence by this are states like Michigan, Missouri, Indiana, Pennsylvania, and Tennessee, moderately large states that would gain the seats if non-citizens weren't counted.

These are constitutional options for reforming the Electoral College while keeping with the principles the founders intended. Is the Electoral College a sure safeguard against the dangers of democracy? No. The founders rightly wanted the will of the people to be reflected in government, even if it bore some risk. But the Electoral College is significantly more effective at preserving our democracy, our republic, and our states, than the alternative.

FAST FACTS

Article II Section 1 of the Constitution is the basis for the Electoral College:

> The executive Power shall be vested in a President of the United States of America. He shall hold his Office during the Term of four Years, and, together with the Vice President, chosen for the same Term, be elected, as follows Each State shall appoint, in such Manner as the Legislature thereof may direct, a Number of Electors, equal to the whole Number of Senators and Representatives to which the State may be entitled in the Congress: but no Senator or Representative, or Person holding an Office of Trust or Profit under the United States, shall be appointed an Elector. The Electors shall meet in their respective States, and vote by Ballot for two Persons, of whom one at least shall not be an Inhabitant of the same State with themselves. And they shall make a List of all the Persons voted for, and of the Number of Votes for each; which List they shall sign and certify, and transmit sealed to the Seat of the Government of the United States, directed to the President of the Senate. The President of the Senate shall, in the Presence of the Senate and House of Representatives, open all the Certificates, and the Votes shall then be counted. The Person having the

64

greatest Number of Votes shall be the President, if such Number be a Majority of the whole Number of Electors appointed; and if there be more than one who have such Majority, and have an equal Number of Votes, then the House of Representatives shall immediately chuse by Ballot one of them for President; and if no Person have a Majority, then from the five highest on the List the said House shall in like Manner chuse the President. But in chusing the President, the Votes shall be taken by States, the Representation from each State having one Vote; A quorum for this Purpose shall consist of a Member or Members from two thirds of the States, and a Majority of all the States shall be necessary to a Choice. In every Case, after the Choice of the President, the Person having the greatest Number of Votes of the Electors shall be the Vice President. But if there should remain two or more who have equal Votes, the Senate shall chuse from them by Ballot the Vice President.

Twelfth Amendment to the United States Constitution, ratified June 15, 1804, amended how the Vice President is selected:

The Electors shall meet in their respective states, and vote by ballot for President and Vice President, one of whom, at least, shall not be an inhabitant of the same state with themselves; they shall name in their ballots the person voted for as President, and in distinct ballots the person voted for as Vice-President, and they shall make distinct lists of all persons voted for as President, and all persons voted for as Vice-President and of the number of votes for each, which lists they shall sign and certify, and transmit sealed to the seat of the government of the United States, directed to the President of the Senate.

States set their own laws regarding how electors are chosen. Twenty nine states and the District of Columbia require their slates of electors to pledge their vote to particular candidates before the election, but

there is no Constitutional enforcement mechanism if the electors break their pledges after they have been selected. Nebraska and Maine award their electors by district rather than winner-take-all.

Republic: "Republic" is a word we rarely hear now outside the Pledge of Allegiance. The American founders considered the republic as the ideal form of government. A republic derives its authority from the consent of the governed, creates laws through elected representatives, and executes laws following due process. The structure of the government was crafted to promote reflection and choice rather than accident and force.

Democracy: In a pure democracy, decisions are made and leaders are chosen by the direct vote of the people. There have been few true democracies in history; the closest approximations were small city states in ancient Greece, but these cities greatly restricted access to voting. Aristotle noted that there may be different uses of the word "democratic," meaning either the things that democracies tend to like or things that tend to promote a continuation of democracy. These may not be the same things. The word "democracy" appears nowhere in either the Constitution, any of its

Amendments, the Declaration of Independence, or even the Articles of Confederation.

Federalism: "Federalism" today refers to the division of power between the states and the central government, located in Washington D.C. Federalism reflects a philosophy, sometimes called subsidiarity, which claims that matters should be dealt with as locally as feasible, both because those closest to the matter probably understand it best and because they are likely in the best position to solve it.

Almost all republics have the word "Republic" in their official title. Think of France, Italy, Germany, or Poland. Our title is the "United *States* of America." States matter incredibly to our federal republican system. The Electoral College reflects that importance.

Absolute Majority: More than 50 percent of the vote.

Plurality: The largest vote total won by a candidate when no candidate wins an absolute majority.

Electoral Majority: A majority of electors in the Electoral College.

Contingent Election: When no candidate receives a majority of the Electoral College, the result is a contingent election decided by a state-by-state (one vote per state) vote in the House of Representatives.

Faithless electors: This is the popular term for electors who don't vote for the candidate who wins the most votes in their state, particularly when the elector had previously pledged to do so.

HISTORY

Congress has decided two contingent Presidential elections in which no one won a majority of electors: in 1800, when Alexander Hamilton aided his old rival Thomas Jefferson in defeating Aaron Burr; and in 1824, when John Quincy Adams won over Andrew Jackson. The Senate decided one vice-presidential election in 1836.

Candidates without an absolute majority of the popular vote won 19 out of 58, or one third, of presidential elections, including Abraham Lincoln, Woodrow Wilson, John F. Kennedy, and Bill Clinton.

Third-party candidates have been awarded electors in 19 out of 58, or one third, of presidential elections and won states in 12 elections, or 20 percent of all elections.

Most states get the president they voted for, with states getting their preferred candidate in office 69 percent of the time.

Five popular-vote winners have lost the presidency, though only one (New York's Samuel Tilden) had an absolute majority. In each of these instances, the candidate who won the presidency had won a majority of the states.

Only five of fifty-eight elections have been won without a majority of states. Two were ties, one resulted in a contingent election, and the other two were won by candidates with a majority of the popular vote.

The 2016 election saw a record number of faithless presidential electors—seven—who voted for five candidates other than Donald Trump or Hillary Clinton (there have been higher defection rates for vice presidential candidates). Five of these faithless electors were Clinton defectors, two registering protest votes for Senator Bernie Sanders and Native American activist Faith Spotted Eagle, the others attempting to start a rush to former Secretary of State Colin Powell as an alternative to Donald Trump.

APPENDICES

Appendices
A – Third-Party Candidates Receiving Electoral Votes
B – How Often States Vote for the Winner
C – State Party Loyalty
D – Elections Won Without Popular Majorities

A: Third-Party Candidates* Receiving Electoral Votes

Election Year	Third-Party Candidates	Electors	States	Candidates' Parties
1808	George Clinton	6	0	Democratic Republican
1824	William Crawford,	41	2	Democratic Republican
	Henry Clay	37	3	Democratic Republican

Election Year	Third-Party Candidates	Electors	States	Candidates' Parties
1832	John Floyd,	11	1	Independent
	William Wirt	7	1	Anti-Masonic
1836	Hugh Lawson White,	26	2	Whig
	Daniel Webster,	14	1	Whig
	Willie Person Mangum	11	1	Whig
1856	John C. Fremont**	114	11	Republican
1860	John Bell,	39	3	Constitutional Union
	John C. Breckinridge	72	11	Southern Democrat
1872	Benjamin Gratz Brown,	18	0	Liberal Republican
	Charles Jenkins,	2	0	Democrat,
	David Davis	1	0	Liberal Republican
1892	James B. Weaver	22	5	Populist
1912	Theodore Roosevelt	88	6	Progressive
1924	Robert La Follette	13	1	Progressive
1948	Strom Thurmond	39	4	States' Rights Democratic Party

Election Year	Third-Party Candidates	Electors	States	Candidates' Parties
1956	Walter Jones	1	0	Democrat
1960	Harry Byrd	15	2	None
1968	George Wallace	46	4	American Independent
1972	John Hospers	1	0	Libertarian
1976	Ronald Reagan	1	0	Republican
1988	Lloyd Bentsen	1	0	Democrat
2004	John Edwards †	1	0	Democrat
2016	Colin Powell,	3	0	Republican,
	John Kasich,	1	0	Republican,
	Ron Paul,	1	0	Republican/ Libertarian,
	Bernie Sanders,	1	0	Democrat,
	Faith Spotted Eagle	1	0	Democrat

* "Third-Party Candidates" is here used as a catchall term for any candidate beyond the top two vote winners who receives electoral votes, regardless of whether they represent a different party, were officially declared candidates, or placed lower than third.

** John Fremont took second in the election, but the Republican Party he ran with was the newest party at the time. Former president Millard Fillmore ran as an American or "Know Nothing" Party candidate endorsed by the formerly major party Whigs. He picked up one state and 8 electors.

† The official name on record is actually "John Ewards," but it is presumed to be a misspelling of Democrat Vice presidential candidate John Edwards.

Data acquired from American Presidency Project presidency.ucsb.edu, cross-checked with the Library of Congress Elections Resource Guides.

B: How Often States Vote for the Winner

State	# of Elections	# Voted for Victor	%
Average			**69.0%**
Median			**69.4%**
New Mexico	27	24	88.89%
Ohio	54	45	83.33%
Illinois	50	41	82.00%
Pennsylvania	58	47	81.03%
California	42	34	80.95%
New York	57	46	80.70%
Nevada	39	31	79.49%
Arizona	27	21	77.78%
Wisconsin	43	33	76.74%
Montana	32	24	75.00%
Indiana	51	38	74.51%
Iowa	43	32	74.42%
West Virginia	39	29	74.36%
Utah	31	23	74.19%
New Hampshire	58	43	74.14%
Missouri	50	37	74.00%
Michigan	46	34	73.91%
Florida	42	31	73.81%
Minnesota	40	29	72.50%

State	# of Elections	# Voted for Victor	%
Oregon	40	29	72.50%
Idaho	32	23	71.88%
Wyoming	32	23	71.88%
Oklahoma	28	20	71.43%
New Jersey	58	41	70.69%
Rhode Island	57	40	70.18%
Colorado	36	25	69.44%
Kansas	39	27	69.23%
North Dakota	32	22	68.75%
Washington	32	22	68.75%
North Carolina	56	38	67.86%
Tennessee	56	38	67.86%
Connecticut	58	39	67.24%
Virginia	56	37	66.07%
Maine	50	33	66.00%
Nebraska	38	25	65.79%
Massachusetts	58	38	65.52%
Louisiana	52	34	65.38%
Maryland	58	37	63.79%
Kentucky	57	36	63.16%
Vermont	57	36	63.16%
Delaware	58	36	62.07%

State	# of Elections	# Voted for Victor	%
Alaska	15	9	60.00%
Arkansas	45	27	60.00%
Hawaii	15	9	60.00%
South Dakota	32	19	59.38%
Texas	41	24	58.54%
Georgia	57	33	57.89%
South Carolina	57	33	57.89%
Mississippi	48	25	52.08%
Alabama	49	25	51.02%
D.C.	14	6	42.86%

C: State Party Loyalty

State	Avg. # of Elections Switching Parties	Avg. Years Between Switching Parties
Average	3.81	52.22
Median	3.43	13.22
Mode	3.00	12.00
New York	2.07	8.30
Wisconsin	2.39	9.56
Colorado	2.40	9.60
Louisiana	2.48	9.90
Nevada	2.60	10.40
Indiana	2.68	10.74
Florida	2.80	11.20
New Jersey	2.80	11.20
Ohio	2.84	11.37
Montana	2.91	11.64
Washington	2.91	11.64
Wyoming	2.91	11.64
Maryland	2.97	11.89
California	3.00	12.00
Hawaii	3.00	12.00
New Mexico	3.00	12.00
West Virginia	3.00	12.00
Iowa	3.07	12.29
Connecticut	3.11	12.44

State	Avg. # of Elections Switching Parties	Avg. Years Between Switching Parties
Rhode Island	3.11	12.44
Tennessee	3.11	12.44
Michigan	3.29	13.14
Kentucky	3.29	13.18
Pennsylvania	3.29	13.18
Missouri	3.33	13.33
Mississippi	3.43	13.71
Delaware	3.50	14.00
New Hampshire	3.50	14.00
Oklahoma	3.50	14.00
Idaho	3.56	14.22
South Dakota	3.56	14.22
Utah	3.88	15.50
Kansas	3.90	15.60
North Dakota	4.00	16.00
Oregon	4.00	16.00
Alabama	4.08	16.33
Illinois	4.17	16.67
Nebraska	4.22	16.89
Georgia	4.23	16.92
North Carolina	4.23	16.92
Massachusetts	4.31	17.23

State	Avg. # of Elections Switching Parties	Avg. Years Between Switching Parties
Arizona	4.50	18.00
Maine	4.55	18.18
South Carolina	4.58	18.33
Virginia	4.91	19.64
Alaska	5.00	20.00
Arkansas	5.00	20.00
Minnesota	5.00	20.00
Texas	5.13	20.50
Vermont	7.00	28.00
D.C.	14.00	--

George Washington not counted; Adams (DR) to Adams (NR) considered consistent loyalty; Jackson (DR) to Jackson (D) considered consistent loyalty; Civil War interruption in voting not counted as a break in loyalty; National Republican and Anti-Masonic to Whig is treated as consistent loyalty; Southern Democrat and Northern Democrat treated as consistent Democratic voting.

D: Elections Won Without Popular Majorities

Year	Pres. Elected	Winner's Vote Share		Runner Up's Vote Share	
		Popular	Electoral	Popular	Electoral
1824*	John Quincy Adams	30.9%	32.2%	Andrew Jackson, 41.4%	37.9%
1844	James Knox Polk	49.5%	61.8%	Henry Clay, 48.1%	38.2%
1848	Zachary Taylor	47.3%	56.2%	Lewis Cass, 42.5%	43.8%
1856	James Buchanan	45.3%	58.8%	John C. Fremont, 33.1%	38.5%
				Millard Filmore 21.5%	2.7%
1860	Abraham Lincoln	39.8%	59.4%	John C. Breckinridge, 18.1%	23.8%
				Stephen Douglas, 29.5%	4%
1876†	Rutherford B. Hayes	47.9%	50.1%	Samuel Tilden, 50.9%	49.9%
1880	James Garfield	48.3%	58.0%	Winfield Hancock, 48.2%	42.0%
1884	Grover Cleveland	48.9%	54.6%	James Blaine, 48.3%	45.4%
1888*	Benjamin Harrison	47.8%	58.1%	Grover Cleveland, 48.6%	41.9%

| Year | Pres. Elected | Winner's Vote Share | | Runner Up's Vote Share | |
		Popular	Electoral	Popular	Electoral
1892	Grover Cleveland	46.0%	62.4%	Benjamin Harrison, 43%,	32.7%
				James Weaver, 8.5%	5%
1912	Woodrow Wilson	41.8%	81.9%	Theodore Roosevelt, 27.4%	16.6%
				William Taft, 23.2%	1.5%
1916	Woodrow Wilson	49.2%	52.2%	Charles Hughes, 46.1%	47.8%
1948	Harry Truman	49.6%	57.1%	Thomas Dewey, 45.1%,	35.6%,
				Strom Thurmond, 2.4%	7.3%
1960	John F. Kennedy	49.7%	56.3%	Richard Nixon, 49.6%	40.7%
1968	Richard Nixon	43.4%	55.9%	Hubert Humphrey, 42.7%	35.5%,
				George Wallace, 13.5%	8.6%

Year	Pres. Elected	Winner's Vote Share		Runner Up's Vote Share	
		Popular	Electoral	Popular	Electoral
1992	Bill Clinton	43.01%	68.8%	George H. W. Bush, 37.5%,	31.2%
				Ross Perot 18.91%	0%
1996	Bill Clinton	49.2%	70.4%	Bob Dole, 40.7%,	29.6%
				Ross Perot, 8.4%	0%
2000*	George W. Bush	47.9%	50.4%	Al Gore, 48.4%	49.4%
2016*	Donald Trump	46.1%	56.5%	Hillary Clinton, 48.2%	42.2%

* Elections won by candidates without a popular vote plurality
† Election won against candidate with absolute popular majority

Data acquired from American Presidency Project presidency.ucsb.edu, cross-checked with the Library of Congress Elections Resource Guides

ACKNOWLEDGEMENTS

My thanks to Thomas H. Patrick for inspiring this project and providing the resources to make it feasible. I must also thank King's College President Gregory Thornbury for recommending I take on this project and King's Vice-President Kimberly Thornbury for shepherding this book through the publication process. King's Presidential Scholar Amity Shlaes provided the impetus and significant guidance along the way.

I am honored that Scott Rasmussen offered his feedback on this book while it was in progress. David Pietrusza, elections historian and walking encyclopedia, offered valuable feedback that improved this book. Dr. Matthew Parks provided many examples and access to his extensive library of primary sources. Dr. Philip Williams advised me on statistics and Dr. Dami Kabiawu's Excel prowess saved me time and helped preserve accuracy.

Thank you to my debate students with whom I've discussed this project. Your probing questions helped me articulate my points more clearly and accurately.

My father-in-law, Dr. David DeJong, proved a valuable editor, as did my sister Esther Daniels.

Finally, I must thank my wife, Rachelle, my first editor and main encourager. This book would not have been possible without her support and the writing is better for it.

ABOUT THE AUTHOR

Josiah Peterson is the debate coach and an adjunct instructor of Argumentation and Debate at The King's College, where he has also taught History of Economic Thought and Persuasive Writing and Speaking. He has assisted Presidential Scholar Amity Shlaes with three courses on The Great Depression, The Great Society, and Calvin Coolidge.

Josiah earned his M.A. in Liberal Studies: Social Sciences at St. John's University, where he served as an assistant debate coach. He earned his B.A. in Politics, Philosophy, and Economics at The King's College, where he competed as a debater.

He served as a research assistant to Scott Rasmussen in his recent book *Politics Has Failed, America Will Not.*

He lives in Brooklyn with his wife, Rachelle, who is also a graduate of The King's College.